Sentences for Vowel Pairs/Digraphs

Author . . . . Marsha Elyn Wright
Editor . . . . Kathy Rogers
Cover Design . . . . Ken Tunell

Table of Contents

Introduction 2

Vowel Pairs/Digraphs

–ai– (long a)................................. 3–5
–ay– (long a) 6–7
–ei– (long a).................................... 8
Review –ai–, –ay–, and –ei–.......... 9–10

–ie– (long i) 11
–ue– (long u) 12
Review –ie– and –ue– 13

–ea– (long e) 14–16
Review –ea– 17–18

–ee– (long e) 19–22
Review –ee– 23–24

–oe– (long o) 25
–oa– (road).............................. 26–27
Review –oe– and –oa– 28–29

–au– (irregular vowel pair) 30
–aw– (irregular vowel pair) 31
Review –au– and –aw– 32

–ea– (bread)............................. 33–34
Review –ea– 35

–oo– (boot) 36–39
Review –oo– 40–41

–oo– (book) 42–43
Review –oo– 44–45

–ow– (snow).............................. 46–47
Review –ow– 48

Reproducible for classroom use only.
Not for use by an entire school or school system.
EP195 • ©2003 Edupress, Inc.™ • P.O. Box 883 • Dana Point, CA 92629
www.edupressinc.com
ISBN 1-56472-195-7
Printed in USA

Introduction

Teachers know that phonics is an important part of literacy instruction. By introducing children to phonetically spelled words and word families, blends, digraphs, r-controlled vowels, vowel pairs (vowel digraphs), and diphthongs, they begin to recognize familiar spelling patterns. They learn to decode by analogy. They develop a store of instant words and learn how to use patterns in familiar words to decode and spell hundreds of unfamiliar words. With this approach to phonics, children become better readers.

Teachers also know that writing is the other necessary part of literacy instruction. As children become better readers, they become better writers!

Sentences for Vowel Pairs/Digraphs uses a phonics-based writing approach to build better readers and writers. This book has over 40 step-by-step activities that combine phonics and writing practice. Every page provides students with the following:

- **Word Bank based on phonetically regular words**
- **Lines on which students write four words from the Word Bank**
- **Space for student illustrations**
- **Sentence frame for students to complete**
- **Lines for students to copy a sentence or write a sentence of their own**

The activity pages can be used in a variety of ways:

- **Introduce (or review) a specific phonics skill or word family**—List the individual words on the board and discuss each word and its meaning. Have each student choose four words from the Word Bank and draw a picture of each within the boxes provided. Then have students write each word under its picture. Instruct students to copy the first sentence given. Have students complete the second sentence by using one or more words from the Word Bank. Then have each student use words from the Word Bank to write an original sentence.

- **Use as a resource for your classroom Word Wall**—Use a thick marker to write the words from the Word Bank on separate sheets of colored paper (large enough to be seen from anyplace in the classroom). Cut around the outline of the letters to create a visual image of each word. Post these colorful words in their appropriate places on your Word Wall.

- **Assign independently as homework.**

- **Compile into student-made books for your classroom.**

In this phonics-based writing series, use the companion book, *Stories for Vowel Pairs/Digraphs,* to reinforce the words provided in each Word Bank.

−ai− (long a)

1. Choose four words from the word bank.
2. Draw pictures of the words in the boxes.
3. Write the word under each picture.

Name_____

Word Bank

gain   bait
main   wait
pain   faint
rain   paint
brain
drain

1. Copy the sentence.
2. Use words from the word bank to finish the sentence.
3. Use words from the word bank to write your own sentence.

1. Dad will wait for me.

2. My knee has a

3.

Sentences for Vowel Pairs/Digraphs   ©EDUPRESS, INC.™   EP195

-ai- (long a)

1. Choose four words from the word bank.
2. Draw pictures of the words in the boxes.
3. Write the word under each picture.

Name_____

Word Bank

bail   pail
fail   rail
hail   sail
jail   tail
mail   trail
nail   wail

1. Copy the sentence.
2. Use words from the word bank to finish the sentence.
3. Use words from the word bank to write your own sentence.

1. I had to mail the sail.

2. Put the nail in a

3.

Sentences for Vowel Pairs/Digraphs   4   ©EDUPRESS, INC.™   EP195

-ai- (long a)

1. Choose four words from the word bank.
2. Draw pictures of the words in the boxes.
3. Write the word under each picture.

Name _____

Word Bank

aid   daily
laid   gaily
maid   praise
paid   raise
raid
braid

1. Copy the sentence.
2. Use words from the word bank to finish the sentence.
3. Use words from the word bank to write your own sentence.

1. Daily I sing gaily.

2. Mom paid the

3.

Sentences for Vowel Pairs/Digraphs ©EDUPRESS, INC.™ EP195

-ay- (long a)

1. Choose four words from the word bank.
2. Draw pictures of the words in the boxes.
3. Write the word under each picture.

Name _____

Word Bank

bay   lay
day   may
gay   pay
hay   say
Jay

1. Copy the sentence.
2. Use words from the word bank to finish the sentence.
3. Use words from the word bank to write your own sentence.

1. Lay the hay here.

2. Jay is by the

3.

Sentences for Vowel Pairs/Digraphs

-ay- (long a)

1. Choose four words from the word bank.
2. Draw pictures of the words in the boxes.
3. Write the word under each picture.

Name_____

Word Bank

Ray   stray
way   tray
bray   crayon
fray   away

1. Copy the sentence.
2. Use words from the word bank to finish the sentence.
3. Use words from the word bank to write your own sentence.

1. Do not stray away.

2. Ray has a

3.

Sentences for Vowel Pairs/Digraphs   ©EDUPRESS, INC.™   EP195

−ei− (long a)

1. Choose four words from the word bank.
2. Draw pictures of the words in the boxes.
3. Write the word under each picture.

Name _____

Word Bank

rein neigh
vein neighbor
reindeer sleigh
eight weigh
eighty weight
freight

1. Copy the sentence.
2. Use words from the word bank to finish the sentence.
3. Use words from the word bank to write your own sentence.

1. Weigh the freight.

2. I see eight

3.

Sentences for Vowel Pairs/Digraphs   8   ©EDUPRESS, INC.™   EP195

Review -ai-, -ay-, and -ei-

1. Choose four words from the word bank.
2. Draw pictures of the words in the boxes.
3. Write the word under each picture.

Name_____

Word Bank

faint   may
paint   Ray
rail   away
sail   neigh
tail   neighbor
lay   sleigh

1. Copy the sentence.
2. Use words from the word bank to finish the sentence.
3. Use words from the word bank to write your own sentence.

1. Ray is my neighbor.

2. He will paint the

3.

Sentences for Vowel Pairs/Digraphs © EDUPRESS, INC.™ EP195

Review -ai-, -ay-, and -ei-

1. Choose four words from the word bank.
2. Draw pictures of the words in the boxes.
3. Write the word under each picture.

Name _____

Word Bank

braid   Jay
maid   pay
bait   eight
wait   eighty
bay   weigh
hay   weight

1. Copy the sentence.
2. Use words from the word bank to finish the sentence.
3. Use words from the word bank to write your own sentence.

1. The maid has a braid.

2. Pay Jay for the

3.

Sentences for Vowel Pairs/Digraphs   10   ©EDUPRESS, INC.™   EP195

-ie- (long i)

1. Choose four words from the word bank.
2. Draw pictures of the words in the boxes.
3. Write the word under each picture.

Name_____

Word Bank

die   dried
lie   fried
pie   tried
tie   fliers
cried   pliers

1. Copy the sentence.
2. Use words from the word bank to finish the sentence.
3. Use words from the word bank to write your own sentence.

1. I tried the fried fish.

2. He got pie on his

3.

Sentences for Vowel Pairs/Digraphs

1. Choose four words from the word bank.
2. Draw pictures of the words in the boxes.
3. Write the word under each picture.

Name _____

−ue− (long u)

Word Bank

cue	duel
due	fuel
hue	cruel
Sue	gruel
clue	true
glue	

1. Copy the sentence.
2. Use words from the word bank to finish the sentence.
3. Use words from the word bank to write your own sentence.

1. We ate some gruel.

2. Give the glue to

3.

Sentences for Vowel Pairs/Digraphs   12   ©EDUPRESS, INC.™   EP195

Review -ie- and -ue-

Name _____

1. Choose four words from the word bank.
2. Draw pictures of the words in the boxes.
3. Write the word under each picture.

Word Bank

pie   Sue
tie   clue
cried   glue
dried   true
fried   fuel
tried   gruel

1. Copy the sentence.
2. Use words from the word bank to finish the sentence.
3. Use words from the word bank to write your own sentence.

1. The glue dried.

2. Sue tried some

3.

Sentences for Vowel Pairs/Digraphs   ©EDUPRESS, INC.™   EP195

−ea− (long e)

1. Choose four words from the word bank.
2. Draw pictures of the words in the boxes.
3. Write the word under each picture.

Name _____

Word Bank

bean   eat
Dean   heat
lean   meat
mean   neat
clean   seat
beat   treat

1. Copy the sentence.
2. Use words from the word bank to finish the sentence.
3. Use words from the word bank to write your own sentence.

1. Dean needs to clean.

2. We will eat a

3.

Sentences for Vowel Pairs/Digraphs   14   ©EDUPRESS, INC.™   EP195

−ea− (long e)

1. Choose four words from the word bank.
2. Draw pictures of the words in the boxes.
3. Write the word under each picture.

Name_____

Word Bank

pea   weak
sea   deal
tea   heal
beak   meal
leak   real
peak   seal

1. Copy the sentence.
2. Use words from the word bank to finish the sentence.
3. Use words from the word bank to write your own sentence.

1. This meal is a deal.

2. I see a seal in the

3.

Sentences for Vowel Pairs/Digraphs   ©EDUPRESS, INC.™   EP195

−ea− (long e)

1. Choose four words from the word bank.
2. Draw pictures of the words in the boxes.
3. Write the word under each picture.

Name _____

Word Bank

each   heap
reach   leap
teach   bead
bleach lead
beam   read
team   leaf

1. Copy the sentence.
2. Use words from the word bank to finish the sentence.
3. Use words from the word bank to write your own sentence.

1. Leap over the heap.

2. I can reach the

3.

Sentences for Vowel Pairs/Digraphs

Review -ea-

1. Choose four words from the word bank.
2. Draw pictures of the words in the boxes.
3. Write the word under each picture.

Name_____

Word Bank

Dean   sea
lean   tea
eat   leaf
meat   bead
real   lead
seal   read

1. Copy the sentence.
2. Use words from the word bank to finish the sentence.
3. Use words from the word bank to write your own sentence.

1. Dean is very lean.

2. I like to eat

3.

Sentences for Vowel Pairs/Digraphs   17   ©EDUPRESS, INC.™   EP195

Review -ea-

1. Choose four words from the word bank.
2. Draw pictures of the words in the boxes.
3. Write the word under each picture.

Name _____

Word Bank

bean   deal
clean heal
heat   meal
seat   beam
beak   team
weak   each

1. Copy the sentence.
2. Use words from the word bank to finish the sentence.
3. Use words from the word bank to write your own sentence.

1. Each team gets a meal.

2. I want a clean

3.

Sentences for Vowel Pairs/Digraphs   18   ©EDUPRESS, INC.™   EP195

-ee- (long e)

1. Choose four words from the word bank.
2. Draw pictures of the words in the boxes.
3. Write the word under each picture.

Name_____

Word Bank

bee   seep
beep weep
deep creep
jeep seem
peep seen

1. Copy the sentence.
2. Use words from the word bank to finish the sentence.
3. Use words from the word bank to write your own sentence.

1. Make the jeep creep.

2. I have seen a

3.

Sentences for Vowel Pairs/Digraphs   ©EDUPRESS, INC.™   EP195

1. Choose four words from the word bank.
2. Draw pictures of the words in the boxes.
3. Write the word under each picture.

-ee- (long e)

Name _____

Word Bank

eel   feet
feel   meet
heel   greet
reel   street
steel

1. Copy the sentence.
2. Use words from the word bank to finish the sentence.
3. Use words from the word bank to write your own sentence.

1. Reel in the eel.

2. Meet me by the

3.

Sentences for Vowel Pairs/Digraphs

-ee- (long e)

1. Choose four words from the word bank.
2. Draw pictures of the words in the boxes.
3. Write the word under each picture.

Name_____

Word Bank

deed   weed
feed   greed
need   fee
reed   flee
seed

1. Copy the sentence.
2. Use words from the word bank to finish the sentence.
3. Use words from the word bank to write your own sentence.

1. I need to feed my cat.

2. Pull out the

3.

Sentences for Vowel Pairs/Digraphs

−ee− (long e)

1. Choose four words from the word bank.
2. Draw pictures of the words in the boxes.
3. Write the word under each picture.

Name _____

Word Bank

peek   greed
seek   cheese
creek   geese
freed   queen

1. Copy the sentence.
2. Use words from the word bank to finish the sentence.
3. Use words from the word bank to write your own sentence.

1. Geese are in a creek.

2. The queen ate

3.

Sentences for Vowel Pairs/Digraphs   22   ©EDUPRESS, INC.™   EP195

Review -ee-

1. Choose four words from the word bank.
2. Draw pictures of the words in the boxes.
3. Write the word under each picture.

Name_____

Word Bank

bee   eel
deep   feel
peep   feed
creek seed
peek   geese
seek   cheese

1. Copy the sentence.
2. Use words from the word bank to finish the sentence.
3. Use words from the word bank to write your own sentence.

1. The creek is deep.

2. Peek at the

3.

Sentences for Vowel Pairs/Digraphs

Review -ee-

1. Choose four words from the word bank.
2. Draw pictures of the words in the boxes.
3. Write the word under each picture.

Name _____

Word Bank

beep   reel
jeep   steel
seem   need
seen   reed
meet   weed
greet   queen

1. Copy the sentence.
2. Use words from the word bank to finish the sentence.
3. Use words from the word bank to write your own sentence.

1. Beep went the jeep.

2. Let us meet the

3.

Sentences for Vowel Pairs/Digraphs   24   ©EDUPRESS, INC.™   EP195

-oe- (long o)

1. Choose four words from the word bank.
2. Draw pictures of the words in the boxes.
3. Write the word under each picture.

Name_____

Word Bank

doe   roe
foe   toe
hoe   woe
Joe

1. Copy the sentence.
2. Use words from the word bank to finish the sentence.
3. Use words from the word bank to write your own sentence.

1. Joe saw a doe.

2. The hoe hurt my

3.

Sentences for Vowel Pairs/Digraphs ©EDUPRESS, INC.™ EP195

-oa- (road)

1. Choose four words from the word bank.
2. Draw pictures of the words in the boxes.
3. Write the word under each picture.

Name _____

Word Bank

oak   float
oat   foam
boat   roam
coat   soak
goat   soap
moat   coach

1. Copy the sentence.
2. Use words from the word bank to finish the sentence.
3. Use words from the word bank to write your own sentence.

1. A boat is in the moat.

2. The goat ate my

3.

Sentences for Vowel Pairs/Digraphs   26   ©EDUPRESS, INC.™   EP195

-oa- (road)

1. Choose four words from the word bank.
2. Draw pictures of the words in the boxes.
3. Write the word under each picture.

Name_____

Word Bank

load   loan
road   moan
toad   groan
coal   roast
foal   toast
goal   cloak

1. Copy the sentence.
2. Use words from the word bank to finish the sentence.
3. Use words from the word bank to write your own sentence.

1. Load the coal.

2. A toad is in the

3.

Sentences for Vowel Pairs/Digraphs   27   ©EDUPRESS, INC.™   EP195

Review -oe- and -oa-

1. Choose four words from the word bank.
2. Draw pictures of the words in the boxes.
3. Write the word under each picture.

Name _____

Word Bank

doe   load
hoe   road
Joe   toad
oat   loan
boat   moan
coat   groan

1. Copy the sentence.
2. Use words from the word bank to finish the sentence.
3. Use words from the word bank to write your own sentence.

1. Loan me your coat.

2. I hear Joe

3.

Review -oe- and -oa-

1. Choose four words from the word bank.
2. Draw pictures of the words in the boxes.
3. Write the word under each picture.

Name _____

Word Bank

foe   roast
roe   toast
goat   coal
float foal
soak   goal
soap   coach

1. Copy the sentence.
2. Use words from the word bank to finish the sentence.
3. Use words from the word bank to write your own sentence.

1. This soap can float.

2. The coach eats

3.

Sentences for Vowel Pairs/Digraphs

-au- (irregular vowel pair)

1. Choose four words from the word bank.
2. Draw pictures of the words in the boxes.
3. Write the word under each picture.

Name _____

Word Bank

auto   author
autumn caution
haul   caught
maul   because
sauce   daughter

1. Copy the sentence.
2. Use words from the word bank to finish the sentence.
3. Use words from the word bank to write your own sentence.

1. I like hot sauce.

2. He will haul the

3.

Sentences for Vowel Pairs/Digraphs   30   ©EDUPRESS, INC.™   EP195

-aw- (irregular vowel pair)

1. Choose four words from the word bank.
2. Draw pictures of the words in the boxes.
3. Write the word under each picture.

Name_____

Word Bank

jaw   lawn
paw   yawn
raw   claw
saw   straw
dawn   crawl
fawn   hawk

1. Copy the sentence.
2. Use words from the word bank to finish the sentence.
3. Use words from the word bank to write your own sentence.

1. I saw a fawn at dawn.

2. I will crawl in the

3.

Sentences for Vowel Pairs/Digraphs ©EDUPRESS, INC.™ EP195

Review -au- and -aw-

1. Choose four words from the word bank.
2. Draw pictures of the words in the boxes.
3. Write the word under each picture.

Name_____

Word Bank

auto	jaw
autumn	saw
sauce	fawn
caught	lawn
because	crawl
daughter	hawk

1. Copy the sentence.
2. Use words from the word bank to finish the sentence.
3. Use words from the word bank to write your own sentence.

1. A girl is a daughter.

2. I saw a

3.

Sentences for Vowel Pairs/Digraphs

-ea- (bread)

1. Choose four words from the word bank.
2. Draw pictures of the words in the boxes.
3. Write the word under each picture.

Name_____

Word Bank

head   bread
lead   spread
read   thread
breath meadow

1. Copy the sentence.
2. Use words from the word bank to finish the sentence.
3. Use words from the word bank to write your own sentence.

1. I read about lead.

2. I like to eat _____

3.

Sentences for Vowel Pairs/Digraphs   ©EDUPRESS, INC.™   EP195

-ea- (bread)

1. Choose four words from the word bank.
2. Draw pictures of the words in the boxes.
3. Write the word under each picture.

Name _____

Word Bank

heavy   feather
ready   leather
steady   sweater
measure weather
treasure

1. Copy the sentence.
2. Use words from the word bank to finish the sentence.
3. Use words from the word bank to write your own sentence.

1. The weather is cold.

2. I will put on a

3.

Sentences for Vowel Pairs/Digraphs 34 ©EDUPRESS, INC.™ EP195

Review -ea-

1. Choose four words from the word bank.
2. Draw pictures of the words in the boxes.
3. Write the word under each picture.

Name_____

Word Bank

head   meadow
lead   heavy
read   ready
bread   feather
spread sweater
thread weather

1. Copy the sentence.
2. Use words from the word bank to finish the sentence.
3. Use words from the word bank to write your own sentence.

1. Pull the heavy thread.

2. Put jam on my

3.

Sentences for Vowel Pairs/Digraphs   35   ©EDUPRESS, INC.™   EP195

-oo- (boot)

1. Choose four words from the word bank.
2. Draw pictures of the words in the boxes.
3. Write the word under each picture.

Name _____

Word Bank

cool   boom
fool   doom
tool   loom
food   room
mood   zoom

1. Copy the sentence.
2. Use words from the word bank to finish the sentence.
3. Use words from the word bank to write your own sentence.

1. That tool is cool.

2. Zoom into that

3.

Sentences for Vowel Pairs/Digraphs   36   ©EDUPRESS, INC.™   EP195

-oo- (boot)

1. Choose four words from the word bank.
2. Draw pictures of the words in the boxes.
3. Write the word under each picture.

Name_____

Word Bank

too   boot
zoo   hoot
drool   loot
school root
spool   toot
stool

1. Copy the sentence.
2. Use words from the word bank to finish the sentence.
3. Use words from the word bank to write your own sentence.

1. A boot is on the stool.

2. I went to the

3.

Sentences for Vowel Pairs/Digraphs   37   ©EDUPRESS, INC.™   EP195

-oo- (boot)

1. Choose four words from the word bank.
2. Draw pictures of the words in the boxes.
3. Write the word under each picture.

Name _____

Word Bank

hoop   troop
loop   bloom
droop   roof
stoop   shoot
swoop   tooth

1. Copy the sentence.
2. Use words from the word bank to finish the sentence.
3. Use words from the word bank to write your own sentence.

1. I see the bloom droop.

2. I lost a

3.

Sentences for Vowel Pairs/Digraphs   38   ©EDUPRESS, INC.™   EP195

-oo- (boot)

1. Choose four words from the word bank.
2. Draw pictures of the words in the boxes.
3. Write the word under each picture.

Name_____

Word Bank

moon   scoop
noon   goose
soon   loose
spoon moose
snooze rooster

1. Copy the sentence.
2. Use words from the word bank to finish the sentence.
3. Use words from the word bank to write your own sentence.

1. The goose is loose.

2. Soon I will see a

3.

Sentences for Vowel Pairs/Digraphs   39   ©EDUPRESS, INC.™   EP195

Review -oo-

1. Choose four words from the word bank.
2. Draw pictures of the words in the boxes.
3. Write the word under each picture.

Name _____

Word Bank

cool   droop
tool   stoop
boom   roof
room   moon
zoo   spoon
boot   rooster

1. Copy the sentence.
2. Use words from the word bank to finish the sentence.
3. Use words from the word bank to write your own sentence.

1. This rooster is cool.

2. Let us go to the

3.

Sentences for Vowel Pairs/Digraphs   40   ©EDUPRESS, INC.™   EP195

Review -oo-

1. Choose four words from the word bank.
2. Draw pictures of the words in the boxes.
3. Write the word under each picture.

Name _____

Word Bank

food   troop
mood   bloom
school tooth
stool   goose
root   loose
toot   moose

1. Copy the sentence.
2. Use words from the word bank to finish the sentence.
3. Use words from the word bank to write your own sentence.

1. This is a school stool.

2. I see a loose

3.

Sentences for Vowel Pairs/Digraphs   41   ©EDUPRESS, INC.™   EP195

-oo- (book)

1. Choose four words from the word bank.
2. Draw pictures of the words in the boxes.
3. Write the word under each picture.

Name _____

Word Bank

book   boor
cook   poor
hook   foot
look   cookies
took

1. Copy the sentence.
2. Use words from the word bank to finish the sentence.
3. Use words from the word bank to write your own sentence.

1. Look at this book.

2. I took the

3.

Sentences for Voxwel Pairs/Digraphs

-oo- (book)

Name _____

1. Choose four words from the word bank.
2. Draw pictures of the words in the boxes.
3. Write the word under each picture.

Word Bank

good   hoof
hood   brook
wood   crook
stood shook
wool

1. Copy the sentence.
2. Use words from the word bank to finish the sentence.
3. Use words from the word bank to write your own sentence.

1. My hood is wool.

2. I stood in the

3.

Sentences for Vowel Pairs/Digraphs   43   ©EDUPRESS, INC.™   EP195

Review -oo-

1. Choose four words from the word bank.
2. Draw pictures of the words in the boxes.
3. Write the word under each picture.

Name_____

Word Bank

book good
cook stood
hook brook
foot crook
cookies

1. Copy the sentence.
2. Use words from the word bank to finish the sentence.
3. Use words from the word bank to write your own sentence.

1. The cookies are good.

2. I stood on one

3.

Sentences for Vowel Pairs/Digraphs

Review -oo-

1. Choose four words from the word bank.
2. Draw pictures of the words in the boxes.
3. Write the word under each picture.

Name_____

Word Bank

look   wood
took   wool
boor   hoof
poor   shook
hood

1. Copy the sentence.
2. Use words from the word bank to finish the sentence.
3. Use words from the word bank to write your own sentence.

1. We took a look.

2. He shook his

3.

Sentences for Vowel Pairs/Digraphs

-ow- (snow)

1. Choose four words from the word bank.
2. Draw pictures of the words in the boxes.
3. Write the word under each picture.

Name_____

Word Bank

bow grow
low pillow
mow yellow
row snow
crow snowman

1. Copy the sentence.
2. Use words from the word bank to finish the sentence.
3. Use words from the word bank to write your own sentence.

1. I have a yellow bow.

2. I will play in the

3.

Sentences for Vowel Pairs/Digraphs ©EDUPRESS, INC.™ EP195

-ow- (snow)

1. Choose four words from the word bank.
2. Draw pictures of the words in the boxes.
3. Write the word under each picture.

Name_____

Word Bank

blow   narrow
flow   below
glow   bowl
slow   rainbow
arrow   window

1. Copy the sentence.
2. Use words from the word bank to finish the sentence.
3. Use words from the word bank to write your own sentence.

1. This arrow is narrow.

2. I see a

3.

Sentences for Vowel Pairs/Digraphs 47 ©EDUPRESS, INC.™ EP195

Review -ow-

1. Choose four words from the word bank.
2. Draw pictures of the words in the boxes.
3. Write the word under each picture.

Name _____

Word Bank

bow   arrow
low   narrow
mow   pillow
row   yellow
crow rainbow
grow window

1. Copy the sentence.
2. Use words from the word bank to finish the sentence.
3. Use words from the word bank to write your own sentence.

1. Mow the row of corn.

2. Look out the _____

3.

Sentences for Vowel Pairs/Digraphs